DREAMS

DEBRA SARASWATI SIMPSON

outskirts
press

Outskirts Press, Inc.
http://www.outskirtspress.com

Paperback ISBN: 978-1-9772-6989-8
Hardback ISBN: 978-1-9772-6990-4

Library of Congress Control Number: 2023922667

Author Photo © 2024 Johnnie Simpson. All rights reserved - used with permission.
Cover Photo © 2024 Debra Saraswati Simpson. All rights reserved - used with permission.

Outskirts Press and the "OP" logo are trademarks belonging to Outskirts Press, Inc.

PRINTED IN THE UNITED STATES OF AMERICA

I dedicate this book
to Johnnie Simpson,
my husband, forever love,
best friend, soulmate, and muse.
I love you.

THANK YOU to my family and friends for always encouraging me to write, and to dream.

- Johnnie Simpson – my husband, muse, and inspiration.

- Devin, Johnnie, and Rosie – my kids, who always inspire me with their art, writing, and creativity.

- Bonnie Brown, Jessica Ruster, and Ruth Paget (the Three Graces) – my writing buddies and beloved friends.

- Debbie Otto – my best friend for 45 years. Thank you for always believing in me, and for sharing adventures.

- David Gitin – my writing teacher, gifted poet, and friend.

- Nadjet and Paul Kob, and Joe and Sue Boogren – dear friends, partners, and family.

- My family – Nick, Hannah, Alaina, Heather and Randy, Rodney, Barbara and Johnnie Frank, and my parents Lyn and Bob for their love and support.

- Robin Quibilan – my sister and best friend, who inspired two of these poems: "Fallen Chrysalis" and "Grace".

- Teddy, Orion, Arty, and Stella June – my grandchildren. May your most wonderful dreams come true.

Contents

DREAMS

THE MUSE

"We are all wanderers
on this earth. Our hearts
are full of wonder, and our
souls are deep with dreams."
- Romani Saying

PETALS

Solitude

I write within the cloister of my room
and my words glow amber in the candlelight.

My open window invites
threads of light, moon-wings,

while I, concubine to an invisible muse
record the moment faithfully—

    raiment of violets,
    perfume of summer: green,
    and evening,
      drowsy with rain.

Pink Moon

The full moon rises
above the field
of dewy grass

soft light kisses
budding lilacs

in the garden
a drowsy honeybee
sleeps

iridescent wings
on a bed
of shimmering petals

Fallen Chrysalis

In Spring
I planted timothy grass,
milkweed and lavender.
I listened to the waves
of grasses in the meadow,
and tried to save a fallen chrysalis,
lifting gently
a jewel of celadon,
dream of wings.

Morning dew
dotted leaves and buds
glittering in the fragrant garden.
Whispering softly
I cast a spell,
my breath
scattering seeds
on a puff
of dandelion.

Lake Huron

I wake early
after a night of vivid dreams.
Mist rises from the cool lake,
the cedars sparkle
in silver light.

Yesterday I sat with Sue
at her lake house.
Still so beautiful,
she lay in bed holding my hand
as we said goodbye.

My heart is bursting
with all I want to say---
how the past few days have changed me.
Her courage and grace
light this path.

Today I'm back on the road,
sun in my eyes, headed home.
Tomorrow I'll pick up my pen,
wandering the labyrinth,
seeking words, like pearls.

Blessing

Bring me the crescent moon
and pink orchids
on the windowsill
in my small, warm kitchen.

Bring cold November days,
cups of jasmine tea
and sacred trees.

Ornaments
of ordinary days
are gifts of joy.

In each breath
love abides.

Snowstorm

Snow glitters on thin branches
of young trees,
the full Wolf Moon
howls in the wind.

No place we need to be,
we burrow
like foxes
in our den.

The tea kettle whistles
in the cold kitchen,
echoes
like a distant train.

Sensuous kisses,
the warmth of your arms…
Outside, blue light
in the darkness.

Home

Glinting yellow light
traces curves of pink clouds
floating above the hillside.

Fireflies sparkle
like stars
above the warm grass.

We sit on the porch swing
rocking.
The white oak
luminous
in moonlight.

Sunrise

Morning arrives
spreading rose-colored wings
across a silent grey sky.
Fingers of light illumine
the empty field, the silver pond.
The barn is golden like a palace.
I sip oolong tea slowly
in the whispering kitchen,
as the blue butterfly orchid
dancing on my windowsill
unfurls her silky petals,
  swallowing dewdrops,
  reaching for light.

Writing

all day in the quiet house
I listened
waiting for the muse

rain splashed in puddles on the street
as the sky bloomed
violet and indigo

trails of dark ink
   spiraled from my pen

the vase upon my desk
held clouds
   of blue hydrangeas

Illumination

Morning blossoms
upon the horizon

~~a sea of roses
   beyond the shore.

Dewdrops rest on the windowpane,
    remnants of moon.

I awaken to your kiss
as moonflowers slumber,
and stars dissolve
in pearls of light.

Sonoma Moon

the moon spins
threads of silver
& tearoses
glisten with rain

succulent grapevines
shimmer in the vineyard
strands of poetry
on a summer night

the moon
is a flame
dancing
in the wineglass

from this chalice
of moonlight
I sip poems,
roses,
dew

Pink lotus blossoms
floating upon moonwater
willows bow deeply

Japan, Late Summer

I remember the nectar of petals in the air
and the sweet scent of the straw floor in my room
where we met in secret.

Moonlight cast slanting shadows on the wall
and large black crows gazed silently
from dark trees.

We loved the silhouette of bamboo
upon the white paper blocks of the shoji screen
and the sound of the leaves, rustling like rain.

silky peonies
sip pearls of morning dew
sensuous perfume

floating petals, pink clouds
dance in the garden at dawn

dark wings of wild geese
write joyful calligraphy
on the rose pink sky

poems float on the blue pond
music of August twilight

Miyuko

a swish of soft silk,
a scarlet sash

the geisha floats
in the garden
of the temple

along the path
clouds of perfume
rise from white camellias

red poppies dance
beneath
the Bodhi tree

The Geisha Begins Her Story

It is summer in Nikko
and you have returned.

Blue petals of the iris arch
above the shimmering wings of the dragonfly.
Transparent reflections
lean upon the blooming lake.

A flute sings in the humming twilight,
and in the dry bamboo grove
the wind and the leaves
pretend they are rain.

You are the laughing moon.

Kyoto Spring

white roses,
milky white,
clouds of petals
floating

::

a blue dragonfly
dances like a geisha
in the dewy garden

::

mantra
of bees humming

shrine
of chrysanthemum

Cherry Blossom Tree

Muse of spring,
adorned like a goddess,
lifts jeweled branches,
strands of pink petals,
to the lush, fragile light.

In rippling waves of wind,
flowers rustle
like a dress of silk.
Tomorrow
spring breezes
will undress her,
powdering the air
with sighs.

Petals fly away
shimmering like wings.

Brief as dawn,
this April interlude,
remembered like a kiss.

Clouds

The clouds are paper lanterns,
translucent,
as the last rays of sunlight
flicker inside them.

Huge floating peonies
dripping colors
into the sea,
like rain.

We open
to sacred silence,
numinous and beautiful---
the seduction of sunset,
the transformations.

Velvet

We lie in the hush of starlight,
inhale the darkness,
the redolence
of shimmering rain,
and I open to the poem
of your breath,
your golden skin.
Your kisses are roses
blooming
petal by petal.
My lips are crimson,
savoring
every drop
of nectar.

A shrine of bamboo
Light flickers on sapphire wings
Dragonfly Goddess

Meditation

Petals of the peony,
a silk carpet...

hum of the bee,
the only sound
in the silence
of the temple.

Morning Meditations

White hyacinths blossom
in straight rows
in my neighbor's garden.
Sunlight sings softly
on this early spring morning.

::

In the kitchen,
in the corner of the windowpane,
the mandala of a spider's web
shimmers with morning dew.

::

A tiny ladybug
wanders a swirling branch
of the bonsai tree,
a goddess lost
in a sea of green

      one long branch of the juniper, bowing.

A dance in the wind
light and shadow flickering
leaf, or butterfly?

Splash of yellow light
disarray of wildflowers-
impressionist Spring

Summer alchemy
within the temple of bees
chalice of honey

Autumn alchemy~
all day painting this gold leaf
twilight deepening

Poetry of trees
powerful bonsai branches
defining haiku

Scarlet Dragon, Amber Moon

I saw you at the Temple
of the White Horse
when the lush serenity
of Mount Mang
had called us

      our meeting
      was like a memory
      I remember

      and the taste
      of plum wine
      I remember

I imagine you still
out on the river
casting your nets
in the morning mist

in Shanghai
I waited for you
beneath the neon dragon
at the end of Nanjing road

      remember me
      in your tranquil chamber
      I am waiting

      waiting under an amber moon
      dreaming of distant grottoes

Sleeping Beauty

intoxication

the scent of violets
  after rain

night winds ravish
  the sycamore trees

green leaves
  ripple like a stream

at my bedside
  books, poems, spells

words dissolve
  in the mist of dreams

hours fall away
  in the soft rose of night

beneath a tapestry
  of petals and starlight

  I awaken
to the sweet kiss
  of a strawberry moon

Poet

The poet is a nomad
who may hear a crescendo
in the aura of rain.

Wild Dandelions

Wild dandelions
gather with butterflies
beneath the tender willow.
I lie with them
in tall grass,
savoring the light
and textures
of their silence.

DREAMS

Self-Portrait

I stand barefoot
in the kitchen
arranging fruit.

I capture peaches,
sing in red,
worship rain.

And my dream
is to chant
a rose-language---
to sculpt
the glorious ink,

beauty in whispers, or
fiery absurd art.

Outside the daisies shimmy
in the scowling light of noon.

Exile

The evening is topaz
and the light whispers
above the bay.

At my house
the rooms are filled
with the ghost of your cello,
the incense of rain.

In candlelight
I sip
salty books
like broth

and await comfort
in the chaos
of thunder.

Wolf Moon

Winter night~
The west wind
murmurs,
birthing stars.

The sea is in bloom.
I want to sleep
on the glittering
shore.

The goblet is full.
I feel
your breath
on my shoulder.

Tonight
Wolf Moon
illumine
my life.

Fragment of a Dream

I stood naked in moonlight
on a street in Ravenna
and lifted my glass
to three flaming stars.

For too long I wandered
graying streets
in a distant towering city
and my own granite mind.

I was rescued by a kiss
in the plume of night,
the full moon whitening
my empty pages.

I think of Dante,
exile in Paradise.
Here you must sing
to be understood.

Gloria

Soft morning,
softer in Assisi.
Pale dawn ripens
in the olive grove.
A goldfinch sings
in the feathery mist.

Soft morning,
flowing grace.
I walk in the dewy garden
among petals
gathering light.
Sweet persimmons blaze!

I hear the music
of branches,
songbirds, sheep.
This house of light
enfolds me.
I've never tasted figs so sweet.

Grace

In the gauzy texture of soft light,
the great dome of La Fiore
hovers above the city, ethereal.

At dawn, my sister looks out at the Arno,
from her perch upon Ponte Vecchio
beneath a blushing Florentine sky.

For hours she explores the Renaissance city
within a lavender mist
encircling Florence like an aura.

The old streets suffused with the freshness of rosebuds,
the architecture embracing mystery,
the great voices whispering ceaselessly.

So intimate, so near,
she could, almost,
believe.

At the Uffizi
in the late afternoon,
she stands admiring "La Primavera", entranced.

Dreaming, she joins the Graces in the dance,
savoring the faint scent of flowers in the air,
the light above her falling on her Botticelli hair.

La Primavera

spring
dripping
petals
roses
rain

spring
raining
starlight
perfume
mist

a net of stars
caught
in the willow

bouquet of rosewater

baptism
of silky grass

Benediction

rosy lips of morning
kiss drowsy petals
& sunflowers
are resurrected

fluent
in the murmur
of bees
chanting

beehive
field
womb

Trespassing

Lured
by red lacquer cherries
and supple leaves
we walked along
the soft and grassy path.
The orchard was tranquil,
imbued with perfume,
iridescent cherry trees
danced
like painted nymphs,
and the sky blazed scarlet
at sunset.

Dear Marco

The plangent bells of San Marco chime
and I waken in my hollow room alone,
longing to reenter my dreams,
remembering your petal kisses,
the scent of your skin, like nectar,
wrapped in the luxurious gesture of your eyes.
I love you. I loved all our possibilities.
You haven't come in weeks.
With you I threw off the garments of a courtesan,
and loved.
I loved my own name on your lips.

I saw you with her today
in the fragrant air of the Rialto marketplace,
and watched you laugh with her,
and watched you fill her basket with our sweet apricots
and golden pears.
I tried forgetting. I waited for you to see me.
I followed you to the bridge
and when a cat arched its back
and slowly moved away,
you turned.
How do I endure your glance of indifference?

I remember you naked in the breath of sunrise
lying on the disheveled sheets like Neptune
on the waves of the sea...
When you embraced her on the bridge,
a thought, uninvited, filled my body,
and I imagined the rustle of silk,
her dress falling with malicious ease,
your savage kiss.

I returned to my house late tonight,
lost in dreams of you,
the gondola floating on the black water.
The rhythmic breath of the gondolier
was the only sound in the darkness.
Then the call of a nightingale
from its cage above the canal
jangled the voluptuous music of my desire,
mocking my longing.

The faces of palaces
were draped in a veil of moonlight.
We glided on, and reaching your palazzo
I looked up at your window.
The candlelit chandelier
behind the glass
glittered like diamonds.
I heard the soft notes of a piano nocturne,
and watched them ripple on the surface of the water,
enveloped in the redolence of rain and jasmine,
the last song in the night.

A Spell, for my lover

You will dream of Venice
& feel my cheek on your shoulder.

When you speak to her
with your breath of lavender,
my kisses
will bloom
inside you.

At your desk
in shadows
poems will empty you.
Sunsets will leave you
melancholy.
Your friends won't understand.

In bed
night will split you open.

You will remember
every time you see the moon,
and when the rain comes
you'll taste your own salty tears.

A cock will crow
in the winter light
and you will search
an empty mirror
for your reflection.

Remembrance

Whispering your love song softly
in the doorway of the room,
yes you loved me for a time,
where the florid shadows bloom.

Limpid waves of light abandon
hidden chambers where we'd meet.
Arching bridges, lonely windows,
echo voices, indiscreet.

See how fluidly the moonlight
ripples on the darkening sea,
kissing Venice, golden goddess,
temple, starlight, memory.

Lament for a lost lover

then, smiling
you called yourself
vagabond, nomad

and quietly
you promised me
freedom and forgetting

months
I lamented
forsaking everything I thought

belonged to you. I abandoned
that perfume
that brought you back into the room

I deconstructed
came undone
whereupon

I watched your face
evaporate
in a martini

Memory

In dreams
I still see your room,
the light ravishing
the garden outside your window
and the golden sunflowers
bowing
like maidens.

Though I'm not there
I feel the cool tiles
of the mosaic floor,
and in that palace of light
your kisses
tango
across my back.

To Sea

Something in your music reminds me
of the glissando breeze
caressing the willow
that night in Venice.

We floated past it in the gondola
as if in a dream
and when it shuddered
so did we.

I have a photograph of you
sipping chocolate
at Florian's
on a sumptuous autumn night.

In your eyes
there is a boy
who still believes
in dragons and mermaids.

You stood before the lions
at the Arsenale~
a sea-captain,
unmasked.

Last night
I kissed the seafoam
on your lips
and heard the drumbeat of the sea.

You leave me tomorrow.
Tonight
your heart beats thunder
and my tears are rain.

Venezia

Sensuous Venice
shimmering behind your veil of mist
bring me your sapphire music.

Cloak me in your velvet night
as the glistening rain falls gently
like passionate teardrops.

The moon floats in the sky above the piazza
and the little orchestra at Florian's
recalls the poetry of a crimson tango.

I stand beneath the lamplight,
hear the sighs of ancient palaces,
breathe the musty perfume of the goddess.

Not far away, beyond these islands,
Venus reclines on the waves of the sea.

Lost in the clear midnight,
lovers sit cradled among pillows in a gondola,
gliding through echoes of the chanting bells of churches.

From a nearby canal, one luminous voice,
thoughtful as a violin
declares a silky lovesong.

La Serenissima vibrates with joy!

Love Song

I
love
the mirror of you
Venice

I love
the echo of you

I love
your shadows,
reflections,
your music
that keeps repeating

Serene Goddess
Shrine of Light
Moon Lover

drawing breath
from poet's dreams

Ode to Napoli

Goodbye Bella Napoli, I love you!

In the silvery light after the rain,
  smudges of pink and gold adorn
    your pewter blue sky, and you are wild
    and beautiful as a nymph.

I've wandered your tangled streets
  lost in the pungent scent of outdoor markets
    and music of voices, sturdy as thunder,
      embellished with a theater of hands.

The dishabille of laundry stretching
  from window to window above the narrow streets
    feels cozy as a favorite room
      though you are poor and unkempt as an urchin.

Bella Napoli, I miss you.
  Nestling at the foot of Vesuvio, a dusty antique,
    scattered with poppies, reposing by the sea,
      your perfume of lemons and roses, the opalescent light!

You are vibrant and eccentric,
  flaunting your ornaments-
    castles and palaces, churches and theaters,
      like a queen.

I was looking out at the bay
  watching the languorous descent of the sun,
    saturated with longing, plotting my return,
      when I remembered...

In a dream last night
I saw a smiling Pulcinella wink at me
then turn and disappear into the shadows
of the Spaccanapoli.

Amalfi Night

One face of night
in an infinite number of nights.
One powdery moon,
pale and shimmering.
After all other nights
too light to be remembered long,
dissolving.

Yet I remember
how the sea-glass glimmered
like small ruins on the beach,
the silhouette of roses
along the garden wall,
the supple trunks
of young chestnut trees,

and all night
the rain,
chanting music
like a shaman.

Rite

Silence is imposed
at Alberobello.
Too far away
to be Italy.
The long hands of cypresses
reach toward heaven.
Mythological chalk symbols
upon the conical rooftops
of trulli houses
glow
in the flickering starlight.
A shining wisp of the moon
rises
among the stark structures,
organic silhouettes,
white beehives.
I linger
in the austere landscape
and study my photographs
--fragments of time--
while night
distills
the essence
of the day.

In the Dreamtime

A dome of moon rises
above the white ruins:
all night reassembling
scattered syllables
and fragments of a dream.

In fragments of your dreams
a blooming sun wanders
rooftops and flower beds.
Forgetfulness gathers
in this temple of light.

Restoration

This is the road that is paved with echoes.

This is the dream you wake to remember.

When the columns crumble
   the domes ascend.

::

Starlight is marooned in the piazza.

You find yourself
in the prism of time.

::

Above the cove,
this altar of the sea,
the hours melt,
the pines are chanting,
a gull is rising~~

   with a song that sounds
   like a call to prayer
     an hour before dawn.

Summer Rain

On a night of summer rain
I awaken.
Your fingers lie tangled in my hair
and the stars are singing.

I practice patience, watch you sleep.
My eyes love
the moonlight
written on your body.

    silver wings
    voice of the moon
    song of summer night

Oh night full of rain,
deepen me
with the textures
of your silence.

Harvest Moon

moonflowers beckon
    sirens in a sea of green

the breath of petals and lush leaves
    perfume the night

we walk in the magical garden
    our path illumined by moonlight

silver stars scribble lost poems
    upon the violet sky

Voluptuary

Unaware
of the seven deadly sins~
crimson roses
slurping
dew.

Night in Cuma

Starlight
kisses the winsome faces
of moonflowers.
I wander among stones
in this sacred place
among scattered ruins,
and hear ancient voices
whisper
near the lost cave
of the Sibyl.
The fragrance of moist earth
mingles with the breath of the sea.
In the sanctuary, alone,
I am thankful for the blessings
of this night.

Lucca

At the café
among the sirens and the crones,
I transcribe a new landscape and its gestures.

Intoxicated by vaporous light,
forgetting all I know about geography,
arrivals and departures,
I found an oasis,
like a shipwreck finds an island--
    serendipity.

Yesterday the pines were swaying at dawn,
fresh handwriting on an empty scroll.

Tonight, a crimson and saffron sunset.
This whimsical composition should be painted.

And suddenly, evening,
overripe and muddled, bows
to a howling, implacable moon.

I was lost and found shelter
in this beauty and bliss.

Transfiguration

This pale, precise swirl of sunrise,
these mist-shrouded vines--
morning is fierce and uncompromising.
Still, I'm able to retrieve a dream:
(the shadows were buoyant where I stood
 and tossed smudged words into glossy puddles.)
I may wake in a bath of light
hungry for revelations--
or be granted grace instead.

I wanted to photograph the hill towns of Italy,
kaleidoscopic patterns of time--
always a new translation, quest for a new idiom.

I stood at the porta looking in,
decoding the ancient town
that speaks to no one, whispers to all
in decrescendo.
Vapors of morning linger here, like a halo,
as earth is denuded.
Always a vision blossoming,
somehow disassembling:
identity language time

I study the feline curve of a hill below the town--
the hills that link town to town.

At the church a mosaic floor is decomposing.
I am deciphering the dialects of this architecture.
The remnants offer clarity,
translate the rhetoric of chiaroscuro.

Here a plume of cloud
above my shoulder,
an undertow
of moon.

Piazza della Rotunda

I love the kaleidoscopic brilliance
of this Roman piazza,
the light and shadows
on the faces of strangers--
It feels as if the world has gathered here.

A bent old woman is begging
beneath the towering obelisk,
a fortune teller strolls by
wrapped in her plume of colors.
There, beautiful lovers
laugh in each other's arms.

We share this cozy room
enclosed by old walls,
cinematic doorways,
and dusty windows.

Together
we linger
at the foot of the Pantheon,
imagining
the echoes
of her celestial
kiss.

Moon Song

I remember ribbons of gold
upon the desert,

your hand in mine
as you drove our dusty car
towards a Pink Moon
over Marrakech.

The amber sunset
cast flames of light
above the white shoulders
of the Atlas.

We reminisced about nights
in Essaouira,
spoke of the sea
and spirals of stars.

Remember the city
    perfumed with orange blossoms,

echoes of the holy call to prayer,

how the sky surrendered
    to the arms of night.

Reverie

Silver teapots
sparkle like jewels
on low wooden tables
at Café des Epices.
We sit near tall open windows
watching kaleidoscopic colors
of the spice market,
taking rest.

Leaning against saffron pillows
you sip hot mint tea,
the brim of your linen fedora
above your dark eyes.

Long shadows of late afternoon
transform the hour
into a moment caught in time,
a dusty photograph.

Sheer curtains diffuse
light like a trance
in the small room.

How many lifetimes
have we loved each other like this…
    your breath sweet as wildflowers…

    Like a spell
        my dream deepens
            with your kiss.

Desideratum

I have loved you
in all your incarnations
over centuries,
transcending time.

I brought you stories
scented with spices of India,
music of Moroccan drums,
the sensual dances of Spain.

Our bodies shared secrets.
We traded names.

We met upon a bridge in Venice,
and knew.

For a moment once in Dublin
I thought I remembered you.

    Somewhere a tiger waits
    in a jungle of trees…

    Today we savor another dream…

So again I bring you
saffron, sandalwood,
jasmine, wine

the arc of my arms
for the grace
of your eyes.

THE MUSE

To a Poet

Words heady as absinthe
left me stranded
beneath a lamppost
bursting with thunder.

The taste of those words,
immutable, returns
like a recurring dream.

In the curve of evening
I remember violets,
voices, smoke,
and goblets of wine
dancing with the moon.

You return in faded pages,
a cartographer of mystical lands,
mapping journeys for my soul.

I twirl on tiptoe
    along the wingspan
        of your radiant calligraphy.

We meet in crackling firelight,
    your letters
        cooing like a dove.

Dreamreading

I've taken one of your shimmering books,
hidden it in my leather bag
and run away.

I like this kind of possession—
lines distilled, like whiskey on my tongue,
fragments of your longing clutching margins,
your poetry of lost things.

You whisper, and music falls like pearls.
I try gathering your sighs
as the wind blows by like a river.

A street of stars is calling.
These pages smell of ash and rain.
This rare volume…
    labyrinth of dreams and burnished moon.

Invocation

I summon you, muse,
tonight
with the sky singing:
owls, stars and moonlight.

A little black bat
curves low in flight,
riding the dark air,
ebony wings flickering.

There is still a bit of fire
glinting in the cinders,
but I've finished the wine,
the glass holds the scarlet stain.

I love beauty.
Tonight it's heartbreaking to contemplate
the eggshell fragility
of each passing season.

I sift the violet ash.
Outside, the wind
is ravishing
autumn leaves.

I invoke you,
Mother, Muse~
unravel my secret
heart

with earth,
    air,
    water
    fire~~

Goddess, summon me
and let this poem
end
in surrender.

Sea Dream, Mermaid Song

I am more myself here.
I feel the masks descending.
Here I know
liberation
of the sensual,
freedom
of the sacred,
my spirit takes flight,
I am home.
I know one day
they will find me
lying on this beach,
with shells in my pockets
and seaweed in my hair.
The breeze comes
in a spiral dance,
peace
nestles in the trees.

Notebook

Below the dim lantern
of moon,
I lie awake
and contemplate
the poem.
I nestle inside
the body of a word.

Luminous

I touch its nude transparency.

::

Thunderous naked canvas
disavowing language today,
obscuring the least gesture.
Muse, quench this dusty page.

My notes are fragile hieroglyphics
where furtive words are sleeping.

I dream garlands of sentences,
green as life, ripe and overflowing.

A brash sentence emerges,
insolent, ascending,
hoisting the poem
upon its shoulders,
clamoring for breath.
But I hear the wingbeats falling
as it melts upon the page.

::

Labyrinth of language~
I must decipher
my self.

::

Sometimes in tattered notebooks
I still peruse the unused fragments,
like ruins glinting in the sun.

Somewhere
the lyrical word
is brandishing
an expansive timbre,

the immaculate sigh.

Wingbeats

the strangeness of the world
  is beguiling

    I drift far away
      on secret expeditions

        or sip memory
          from a fragile teacup

      ::

I sleep
  upon a staff of music...
    in dreams   I dance
      with a shimmering crow

      ::

seeking lands of lost languages
  this handwriting
    telling travel stories
      in a measure of time

black ink
  drips
    from my fingertips

Peach Pie

The spell is cast.
I slice fresh peaches for pie,
toss juicy pieces with vanilla and cinnamon,
and lick sweet nectar from my fingertips.
Suddenly
I'm shrinking
like Alice
after the vial
of poppy elixir,
peering through a keyhole
in time.

My grandmother appears,
her old kitchen gleaming
in sunlight.
The odor of sticky overripe peaches
fallen on musty leaves,
sifts through the screen door
on a summer breeze.
I'm sitting on the cool linoleum floor
shelling green peas
into a milky white bowl.
My grandmother, humming hymns
like a bee,
peels dusty potatoes
as her black cat smiles
from the windowsill.

The pie is golden now,
bubbling like a cauldron,
the kitchen scented with peach perfume.
I close the tattered notebook,
and my grandmother leans above me,
I feel her soft rosebud kiss
upon my cheek.

Sanctuary

At fifteen,
I fast in the cloister
of the library.
Always the new girl,
restless, alone,
invisible
in a maze of uniforms.
Sister Marina nods to me
from her perch in the sanctuary.

Old books hum upon bookshelves,
the musty, earthy scent
fills the room
like incense
in a temple.
I linger in an aisle
with Dostoevsky,
rustling pages,
fragrant with rain.

Hungry, I gather
all the books I can carry
as the school bell rings.
The pages whisper secrets,
brandishing paper wings.

Wicked Queen

My eyes are hazel colors
and my mirror tells me endless lies.

There are many coats I travel in.
I've wandered alone.

And I have known darkness-
upon my altar, a goblet of light.

In rainstorms, I sip tea,
read the oracle of leaves.

I believe in all goddesses.
I am rarely mysterious.

Moonflowers are my favorite
petals. I worship the moon.

There are poems taped to walls,
and books in every room.

My hand holds a wand.
I look younger from afar.

I'm always in love.
You are my magnificent obsession.

Key West

At dawn, the coconut palm emerges
from the cool dark night
and bids farewell to the moon,
regal as a queen.
Emerald fronds stretch toward the magenta sky,
catching light, summoning the sun.
Heat comes raining upon the sea.

   ::

A fluttering orange butterfly
courting a bright pink hibiscus,
lingers near a wing-shaped petal.

Green leaves shimmy in the breeze
   ~~dreams of summer
      in a ray of sunlight.

Waking From Dreams

a figment of moonlight

white peacocks cross
the scattered remnants
of a dream

you abandon the vessel
notes of a guitar, flickering
relinquishing memory

the voyage lost
your yearning enters

the illusion of rain
as the wind
ravishes all the leaves

the sound is muted
but authentic
the photograph fades

waking, all that remains-
a duel of voices,
another language,
not your own

the stars fade
so too does
this bowl of moon,

the scent of lemons,
the sea-soaked notes
  of the lost guitar

In the Barrio de Santa Cruz
A Pantoum

A flamenco guitar is calling to the moon
on the dimly lit stage of the tavern
Remnants of stars are scattered in the night
The hands of a dancer begin to sing

On the dimly lit stage of the tavern
her shadow flickers on the wall
the hands of Romani are singing
beneath petals of the moon

Her shadow is flaming on the wall
~ from the Alcazar garden, a peacock cries
Beneath petals of moon
Desire begets desire

In the gardens of the Alcazar, a peacock cries
The cante jondo has begun
Desire begets desire
Hear the breath of his hands

The cante jondo has begun
& remnants of stars are scattered in the night
Hear the breath of this hands
The flamenco guitar is calling to the moon

Sevilla

So many hours to dream,
sipping duende in a glass of manzanilla.
Scent of oranges fills the air.
Sunlight overflows.
Shrouded in light and shadow
streets of the city
singing a Solea.

Aphrodisiac

The kitchen is warm
& blooming with spices,
saffron, garlic, cinnamon,
as you stir them slowly
in a copper pan,
golden light falls
on your auburn hair.

Pomegranates
and ripe cherries
cross the table,
colors bright
as a Roma caravan.
Your shoulders
move like music.

You offer
roasted chestnuts
in honey,
another bottle of Bordeaux.
In your room
the holy union
of candles and firelight.

Outside in darkness,
the poetry of rain and leaves,
as heat swirls like smoke
on the wet pavement.

Bring me your body
sculpted in moonlight,
bring me your kiss,
your lips
sweet as wine.

Blossoms

I could not go back to sleep.

Blossoms of lilac
brushed against the window screen,
clouds of perfume
floated above our bed,
the curve of your shoulders
was sculpted
in moonlight.

I listened to your sighs
as you slept, my love.
The stars were so near,
and the summer night
was shimmering.

Willow

In the morning
a spasm of rain
engulfs the garden,
replenishing tender leaves
and fragrant blossoms,
thirsty for fountains of music,
strings of silvery rain.
Roots and tendrils
explore dark soil,
quenched by ripe shadows.
Languid hours
of late afternoon, the
immensity of summer lingers,
overflows.
Then day is slowly dismantled
by waves of gold, cascades
of pink, a blush of rose.
Below scattered, diaphanous clouds,
an old willow tree
with tousled strands of silk
is calling,
beckoning,
one last dazzling
column
of light.

Winter Twilight

a flock of wild geese
crosses the evening sky
with graceful wings

noble as knights
trumpeting their pilgrimage
as the moon rises

the winnowing hum of throbbing wings
echoes in the air
above opalescent maple trees

winter twilight
casts hues of blue
upon the soft curves of the hillside

Awakening

I walk out
in the wet morning
listening
to the leafy wisdom
of trees.

Low tide.
The rocks lie naked
in the fragile light.

A blue dragonfly
rises
in the still air.

In the distance
a sailboat,
song of heron's wings.

I hold a small white daisy
against my lips
as the sun rises
and brings to me
the passion to dream,
the courage to be.

Cathedral, Big Sur

We wake at dawn
in the dusty cabin
as morning sings.

Nesting in soft chairs
on the high veranda,
you pour our tea.

Beams of light
illumine redwoods,
eucalyptus,
columns of trees.

Branches arch above us,
and we hear, among the leaves,
the holiness
of wings.

Waiting for Dusk

There is something about foggy mornings in Monterey,
when the cry of the gulls and the wail of the sea
come rushing in on a morning wind.
Hours melt with the sunrise.
By noon, headed for home, I look forward
to another afternoon with Steinbeck.
Sitting nestled in my chair, I taste the sea.
It comes through the window like a spirit in the air.
Wings beating wildly…the butterflies are trying to get in.
Perhaps they know how cozy it is before a fireplace
waiting for dusk.
Or maybe the daisies and bright jonquils on my sill
have secretly seduced them
pretending at evening that they are the sun.

Reflection

The stars are held in the cupped hands of the sky
like a million diamonds in the gentle hands
of a young goddess. There is beauty, here, at the sea.

The moonlight is held in a warm embrace
on the surface of a shimmering tide.
I listen for your voice--Your art is my joy.

The tide moves in swiftly and sweeps away
my name written in the sand. Then comes to meet me,
and wash me in its kisses.

Ode to a Notebook

Dear Notebook,
you help me gather
inspiration,
words of color and flight,
like a butterfly net!
Adjectives like velvet.
Nouns of stone.
You are the mirror
of my soul.
Faithful friend,
your pages are lined
with honey dust.
You keep my secrets
and remember my songs.
To you, I turn again.
My heart carries
its messages to you.
You welcome
the motion of my pen,
the stain of ink,
and symbols of imagination.
In the night
you call me
to work and dreams.
I answer your supplication
with ferocious
strokes of the pen
or observe your nakedness
timidly.
My voice echoes
within your pages, tenderly.

You help me discover
pure essence,
the rhythm of life,
and the mist of dreams.

Reflections

In a past life
I was a gondolier
leaning upon the water
of Venice.
I knew all her misty corners.

I glimpsed my own
reflection
on the surface of the sea,
and sang love songs
like incantations.

In a dream last night
I was spinning
among whirling dervishes
moving in circles
freed by music.

Voices chanting
with confidence
in the moonlight.
Color raining
near dawn.

I have a photograph
of Johnnie and I
sitting beneath a lemon tree
at home in Napoli
many years ago.

The bright yellow lemons
are suspended like suns
among the dark leaves,
and we hold each other
in the summer light.

Through my window
I watch my children
play together outside,
and my heart leaps
with the sound of their laughter.

When I catch my reflection in the glass,
gratitude comes like a wave.
I celebrate these moments
and I'm happy
to know myself.

Today as I looked
in my mirror
I noticed
the lines of my smile
have deepened.

Debra Saraswati Simpson is a poet, traveler, yogini, mom and grandmother. She fell in love with poetry at Maryknoll High School in Honolulu, Hawaii, in Mr. Mattos' Poetry class. She has studied Poetry, Literature and Creative Writing at Southwestern College in Bonita Vista, California, and at Monterey Peninsula College with poet David Gitin, in Monterey, California.

Debra served in the U.S. Navy for five years as a Cryptologic Technician in Japan and Guam. She lived in southern Italy with her family for eight years finding inspiration and reconnecting with her muse.

She currently lives in Westminster, Maryland with her husband Johnnie.

Printed in the USA
CPSIA information can be obtained
at www.ICGtesting.com
LVHW051219241223
767192LV00001B/23